No More Mr. Vice Guy

TYLER FENECK

Published by Ocean Breeze Books

Printed in the United States

Cover Design by Aaron Handwerker

Photographs by Rachael Dana Robinson

NOTICE
The information in this book is for educational purposes only. It is not intended to be a substitute for the medical advice of your healthcare professional.

DEDICATION

To the best Mother a son could ever ask for. Thank you
for seeing me through the darkest times of my life and for
being such a beacon of pure, positive energy. I love you
more than you will ever know…

CONTENTS

INTRODUCTION

On April 21st, 2011, "Erica," the co-author of my first book, *The Cat and the Comedian*, died peacefully in my arms. It was also my 38th birthday, so it was taken as a sign not to grieve, but to celebrate the 16 years of love and life we shared. For the past nine months, that love was needed more than ever; as that's how long it had been since my best friend and father passed away. Life without him wasn't the same, but without Erica, it would have been worse.

Now they were both gone, and I was broke, unemployed, and living with my mother in Temecula, California; also known as the middle of nowhere. My alcohol and marijuana consumption reached new heights. I stopped working out, and my diet consisted of everything under the sun, leading to the largest weight gain of my physical existence. I wasn't dating, had no friends in the area, or the desire to socialize on any level. Additionally, writer's block set in because the creative process behind *The Cat and the Comedian* was over. Though the feedback was positive when it was released in June of 2011, I was far from being in the right mindset to promote it.

I'm not playing the victim game. I'm well aware we create our own realities. Still, this was a darkness I couldn't seem to overcome, and wasn't sure I even wanted to. Zero hope was seen on the horizon, and my mind was constantly clouded in a haze of anxiety, irritability, anger and depression. For well over two years, I wandered around like a ship without a destination.

Eventually, I got sick and tired of being sick and tired, and realized there was a chance to turn things around before it was too late. I became overwhelmed and infused with the desire to free my self from all vices, get to the root of my problems, and once and for all, achieve health and happiness on a mental, physical, emotional, and spiritual level.

As things gradually got better, I realized others could benefit from what I'd learned, and inspiration for *No More Mr. Vice Guy* was born. That said, the book represents my personal point of view only, and is not meant to be the truth for anyone but me. Additionally, I don't feel I have "it" figured out or that I am done evolving on any level. Awareness wise, I remain open minded and skeptical, and I ask you to do the same in regards to the principles in this book. Don't take my word that they work, find out firsthand!

1 ROCK BOTTOM BLUES

"*H*ow the hell am I ever going to get out of this?*" were the only words that rang through my head on a daily basis. Talk about a midlife crisis – holy shit! Living with my mother at age 38, broke, and no career options on the horizon. I wasn't dating because I hated the way I looked due to my weight gain, which was from drinking and eating a ton, trying to escape the fact that I was living with my mother, broke, and had no career options on the horizon!!

The very concept of working made me sick. And technically, I wasn't mentally capable of it anyway. To say I was depressed was the understatement of the century. I had major brain fog and couldn't focus clearly in any way, shape, or form. My creative drive was non-existent, and I literally dreaded getting out of bed every morning. My sinuses were constantly congested.

I had major blood sugar problems, daily headaches from hell, and horrific heartburn that wouldn't quit.

Making matters worse, death surrounded me in every direction. In the last year, I'd lost my father, my cat, and 5 friends from high school, including 2 ex-girlfriends.

This grim reality provided me with a harsh but much needed wake up call. *Be next in line for a coffin, or turn my life around before it was too late.* Though I obviously chose the latter, I did so in a very non-traditional way. At the time, I never felt or looked worse in my life, yet I refused to get checked out by a doctor or seen by a shrink. Had I done so, I'd have been diagnosed with God knows what, and the only cure offered would be…more drugs. Masking the problem was not the answer. That's something I'd already done successfully for the majority of my life. I needed to get to the root cause. Not to mention, with my addictive nature, I needed to start pill popping like I needed a third nut.

My father went to his grave addicted to alcohol, gambling, excessive eating, and lots of other things. I loved him on many levels, but like any of us, he was far from perfect. It was time for me to shed the negative beliefs and habits that wore off on me as a result of being his official clone my entire life and replace them with ones that served me on a much better basis.

I was determined to find out the truth about health and nutrition as well as the relationship between food and mood. My father and 4 of his best friends died of cancer. Did they have to? The conclusion I came to is that we have all, from a very young age, been bullshitted and brainwashed by multiple billion dollar industries into thinking the things we eat are fine, but in reality, they are the very things that contribute to poor health and lead to our ultimate, untimely demise. This is an epidemic. Everywhere I look, people are mindlessly eating the wrong kind of food because they don't know any better.

However, diet is only part of the equation. Attitude and exercise also play huge roles, and fortunately, one hand washes the other the more you put them into action.

For the record, I've been living the lifestyle I describe in this book for 3 years now. I'm happy to report that my health has rebounded and I've achieved the clarity of consciousness I only dreamed of when living in Temecula. I now live on the beach in San Diego with a six-figure income, have lost 65 pounds, and am back to the same 30-inch waist I had in high school!

Headaches...gone. Mood swings...gone. Blood sugar problems...gone. Heartburn...gone. Depression...gone. How did I do it?

By giving up the vices that were holding me back from my ability to reach my unlimited potential.

However, to get to where I am now, I had to get *WAY* out of my comfort zone. I had to wake up, grow up, take responsibility, and make some *major* sacrifices.

For anyone reading this that has vices or addictions they want to shed make no mistake; reading this book or any other will do nothing for you unless *you* are ready and willing to make it happen. The change must come from *within*, and once it does, it's no longer a struggle to give up the vice because it's something you genuinely want to do. We can all be our own best friends or worst enemies. The choice is ours and ours alone.

2 BATTLE OF THE CENTURY

I started drinking alcohol at a very young age because my father always drank it and I wanted to be more like him. When he'd mow the lawn in the summer, he'd give me a large swig of his beer, and I'd also get a small mug of it on holidays and special occasions. To me, it was like drinking liquid gold. Were my parents purposely trying to corrupt me with destructive, addictive habits that would stay with me for life? No. They were just trying to help me feel good, because alcohol always made them feel good. I take full responsibility for becoming addicted to every vice I discuss in this book, but do feel it's valuable to trace back where one is initially exposed to any substance they intend to shed.

I drank every night in my 20's without exception, but by the time 30 rolled around, it was becoming problematic. For one thing, the amount I'd have to consume to catch a buzz just wasn't worth it anymore. I'd end up face down on the floor many nights, but at least had the good sense not to drive. I learned that from my father, who learned the hard way and was very lucky to come out alive, getting 3 DUIs in his day and totaling multiple cars along the way.

Nevertheless, I managed to find ways of putting myself in jeopardy at my own apartment. Like the time I made hard boiled eggs and passed out cold before they were done. I woke up hours later to the smoke alarm going off, exploded eggs and eggshells all over my walls and ceiling, and an empty spaghetti pot that was burnt to a crisp. Not only did I put myself in jeopardy, but also Erica, and everyone in my building. Another time, I fell asleep after putting water on the stove to boil pasta, and woke up to an empty, charred, Teflon pot and a smoke filled apartment. A third time I passed out with while cooking frozen pizza, and woke up to the smoke alarm going off and a charbroiled hockey puck in my oven.

Alcohol was also taking its toll on me in the form of weight gain and depression. I drank because I was depressed and was depressed because I drank. A no win situation for anyone who plays the game.

So when I hit 30 in 2003, I scaled my alcohol intake back by 50 percent. Now, drinking every *other* night as opposed to every night may not sound like progress to your average ear, but after 7 years, I had over 1000 days sober which is a major cutback any way you slice it. My sobriety would go in spurts, lasting days, weeks, or even months at a time.

My father never believed me when I told him I stopped drinking for any period of time, and it used to bother me, but in the end I realized it was because he didn't believe in himself. In our 37 years of existence together, he was only able to remain sober for 2 consecutive months. I'm not knocking him; I'm just explaining who he was. The truth is most of the habits I picked up from my Dad were very positive. We had a great relationship and I wouldn't have traded him for any other father in the history of the world. It just became clear to me that I had to become my own person, step up to the plate and take some responsibility. And for 7 years, I made it work. The nights I drank, I drank less, and the periods of sobriety I experienced were surprisingly enjoyable.

However, everything changed in March of 2010, when my Dad was diagnosed with terminal cancer. From that moment on, I started drinking every night again. After he was gone, I drowned my sorrows even more. Every night, I'd start off with 3 or 4 glasses of wine with dinner, followed by 2 or 3 HUGE vodka and Red Bulls, and finish the night off with 8 – 10 beers. There would usually be an involuntary nap around 10pm, but I'd wake up about midnight, pick up right where I left off, and continue drinking until 3 or 4 AM.

After two years, I'd had *way* more than enough, and remembered exactly why I originally cut back in the first place. The bottom line about booze was that it messed up my memory and blood sugar, impaired my judgment, made me gain weight, piss all the time, and pass out involuntarily. And on top of that, it's expensive! Alcohol is a poison and a depressant. Period. The long-term negative side effects include heart disease, cancer, and liver failure. The short-term negative side effects include memory loss, bad judgment, and hangovers. In exchange for what? A temporary escape from a reality I couldn't stand? In order to be truly free, I needed to create a reality I didn't want to escape from.

Actually, it was no big deal because I no longer enjoyed the experience of drinking and was ready to make the change. Years ago, I learned a "scaling back" technique from George Carlin, who used it to get off beer and cocaine. Instead of going cold turkey, cut your usage back more and more until it's down to only one or two drinks a day, and then stop completely.

However, *when shedding any vice, it is essential to replace the negative addiction with a positive one.* In the case of alcohol, I chose sparkling mineral water and majorly increased the amount of coffee I was drinking. I know coffee isn't exactly a positive addiction, but compared to my alcohol consumption, it was still a major step in the right direction.

My medical marijuana addiction was also out of control. However, due to my financial situation, it was difficult to obtain. At one point, things got so desperate that I traded a signed copy of *The Cat & The Comedian* for $25 worth of weed. The delivery driver I traded it to turned out to be the owner of the dispensary. He and his wife liked my book so much that they ended up becoming friends and hooking me up with massive amounts of reefer for little to no money at all on a regular basis! The Universe is unpredictable when it comes to the manifestation of strong desires.

I realized I was just trading one vice for another, but would deal with that fact soon enough. Most importantly, I'd achieved my initial goal of cutting back the booze, and within a month, it was totally under control. I also used amino acid therapy to help resist cravings. Amino acids are the building blocks of protein that the body uses to produce mood-enhancing chemicals like dopamine and serotonin. Glutamine and GABA are the two supplements I've used that have turned out to be great allies in this department. Eventually, I weaned myself off them too, but would definitely recommend them initially for anyone that wants to get off alcohol.

Glutamine is a predigested, free form amino acid that stabilizes your brain's blood sugar level so that your mood stabilizes too, making you feel calm and balanced. It's also a primary fuel for the entire immune system. Neurotransmitters are produced less and less the more alcohol and sugar you consume. Glutamine helps replenish that supply, relieving symptoms of depression and anxiety, and helps to control cravings for sugar and alcohol. It is used around the world in addiction and rehab centers.

GABA (gamma - amino butyric acid) is an amino acid derivative and a key inhibitory neurotransmitter. Most of the substances used to relieve anxiety – alcohol, weed, tranquilizers, get their effect by boosting GABA levels in the brain. So it makes sense that it would work as a stand-alone supplement. Some argue it does not cross the blood brain barrier when taken orally, but personally, I've had nothing but positive results with it. It's an excellent stress buster, and a natural way to achieve a calm, tranquil state.

For the record, it was not my desire to stop drinking for the rest of my life. I still drink a few beers occasionally, but it *never* grows to an excessive amount, and the next day I'm right back on track. Moderation is a dangerous game for many people and in the past it was for me as well, but this is where the "growing up" and "taking responsibility" factors come in. *If you aren't strong enough yet, don't go there.* It also has a lot to do with giving up the other vices I describe in this book. The purer your body becomes, the less it wants the poison. I still mark each and every day I drink on a calendar, as well as the number of beverages I consume. That way I can look back at any given year and monitor my progress. But it's especially important in the beginning stages, where you are cutting back your usage more and more.

Perhaps in the future it will make sense to give up alcohol completely, but for now I am totally cool with moderately drinking 2 or 3 percent of the time, versus excessively drinking 50 or 100 percent of the time. I'm extremely happy with the progress I've made and no longer consider it a "vice." There are certain vices that do require complete elimination (like the one I'll talk about next), but those are determined by individual choice and individual needs.

In the end, it's about being stronger and less dependant than you were previously. It takes time to get there so be patient. No one is timing you or keeping track of your progress. *The only person you can't fool is yourself.*

3 THE BIG LIE

I started drinking black coffee at a very young age because my father always drank it and I wanted to be more like him. I remember having my first cup with him and enjoying the "buzz" quite a bit.

As I mentioned, my coffee intake increased when I cut back on alcohol, and was now up to 2 pots a day. However, my body had become so acidic that it wasn't long before it could no longer accept the amount I was pouring down my gullet. Well, that's one way to cut back! It's best to take a gradual route when quitting caffeine to avoid withdrawal symptoms like headaches and fatigue. Over a six-week period, I went from 2 pots to 1, to a half a pot. Then down to 3 cups, then 2 cups, then 1, then none...

I officially gave up caffeine on November 2,

2012, and I can't express how much of a positive impact it has had on my overall well-being. Unlike booze, this is one substance I did feel the need to cut out completely.

Caffeine is a very sneaky drug. It is more commonly abused in this country even than alcohol, and the negative side effects could fill a book. In fact, they have filled several, but no one reads them because they're too busy being in denial about their caffeine addiction! But as someone who was specifically looking for help, the best book I've read on it was *Caffeine Blues* by Stephen Cherniske. It's a real eye opener about the detrimental effect that caffeine has on a physical, mental, and emotional level.

The side effects include adrenal fatigue, reduced circulation, headaches, and irritability. Caffeine also causes overproduction of stress hormones, sleep disturbance and insomnia, decreased melatonin production, dysfunction of GABA metabolism, alteration of serotonin levels, and increased blood pressure. It raises glucose and insulin levels, causing weight gain. It also has a negative impact on general metabolism, stresses the liver, and causes premature aging, as it reduces DHEA levels in the body.

Looking back, it's easy to see that the reason I never stopped before was because of fear. I was afraid I wouldn't be able to wake up or even function properly unless I had my coffee fix in the morning. In the end, I learned that sustained energy comes from proper nourishment and eating well. *Not coffee.*

Many of the so called "studies" that show benefits of caffeine are paid for and funded by the coffee industry, a multi billion dollar industry that does not give a rat's ass about your health or mine. The fact is, Americans alone drink 330 million cups a day, and the average person consumes between 3 and 4 cups per day, every day. That's over 1000 cups a year!

Additionally, commercially grown coffee is one of the most heavily sprayed food or beverage crops in the world, causing herbicides, pesticides, fungicides, and other unwanted chemicals to go straight down the throats of those who ingest it.

The acidity level in coffee is off the charts, which is why people get stained teeth when drinking it regularly, along with regular heartburn.

Decaffeinated coffee is still highly acidic and heavily sprayed. Organic is better than not, but with so many additional side effects, I recommend getting off the stuff altogether.

Caffeine is a psychoactive drug that stimulates the central nervous system and adrenals. You think it gives you energy, but what it really gives you is stress. It creates anxiety, impairs nutrient absorption, takes the sheathing off of nerves, dehydrates you, and in the end, *robs you of energy*, which is why you crash or come down off caffeine if you don't keep ingesting more of it into your system.

The drug, of course, has made its way into a lot more food and beverages these days than just coffee. So called "energy" and "sports" drinks are loaded with them, as are sodas, chocolate, candy, cocoa, and certain teas, including green, black, and iced tea.

Unfortunately, most people go their entire lives not knowing what it would be like to live without caffeine. And coming from someone who drank it daily for almost 40 years, you won't know the full effect it may be having on you until you experience what it's like to live without it.

It is one of the greatest feelings on earth to jump out of bed in the morning feeling naturally wide-awake, and not counting on a drug to do it for me. I now drink 16 ounces of distilled water with 2 tablespoons of Bragg's Apple Cider Vinegar first thing in the morning, and have found that gets me flowing perfectly. It's also extremely alkalizing, excellent at regulating blood sugar, and has numerous other benefits as well.

The best coffee substitute I've tried is Teeccino, which is an organic, caffeine free, herbal, non-acidic beverage that comes ground or in teabag form. Their French Roast flavor tastes very much like the real thing, in my opinion.

I also drink a number of caffeine free, herbal, organic teas, and have been blown away by the incredibly tasty offerings they provide as well as the many medicinal benefits. Some of my favorites are Oat Straw, Lemongrass, Catnip, Lavender, Lemon Balm, Hops, Valerian, Horsetail, Rose, and Horehound. Medicinally, I've found Cleavers, Chaparral, Red Clover, Dandelion, and Mullein to be very therapeutic and healing, as they are very alkalizing and great detoxifiers as well.

Kava Kava and Ashwaganda have been big players too and are much more natural, organic, herbal concoctions that give you a nice mellow buzz without side effects.

If you feel that you still need more pep, consider an herbal remedy like a non-ephedrine energy pill. Personally, I found no need for it, due to the incorporation of exercise, breathing techniques, and meditation into my lifestyle.

Of course, I realize there is the social aspect of coffee to consider. It's very ritualistic for most people, and there's a Starbucks on just about every corner to make it easier than ever for people to obtain their fixes. But there are plenty of healthy alternatives to consider, as mentioned in this chapter.

All I can tell you is that I was experiencing a *major* lack of clarity when I started down this path. Brain fog, lethargy, depression, anxiety, and heartburn were 5 attributes I could count on having every day. They are now all but a memory, and a huge part of the reason why is because I'm caffeine free.

4 SUGAR ME TIMBERS

The next vice I decided to take on was one I had been addicted to for the majority of my life. Long before my first taste of alcohol or caffeine, someone in my family celebrated a birthday. I was given a slice of cake, became addicted to sugar, and the rest is history.

99.9 percent of people reading this are currently in the same boat. It's not our parents' fault. After all, they became addicts as children too, and the tragedy continues as I write this today.

The multi billion-dollar sugar industry has done an excellent job of saturating us with this toxic poison over the years. Sugar is in almost *everything* because it's addictive and companies want you consuming their food over and over. From a business perspective, it's brilliant. From a health perspective, it's killing us.

Sugar, like, caffeine, alcohol, or any other drug, is a psychotropic. It is a substance you put in your body that modifies your perception. It's not as dramatic as cocaine or heroin, but it does modify your central nervous system. Initially, it hypes you up. Then it crashes you. To keep up the hype, you ingest more and more. Over time, we get used to sugar and build up a tolerance. It doesn't mean it no longer has an effect. It means that a foggy state of mind has now become normal. *What most people don't know is what it's like to have a clear state of mind!*

Sugar is also a controller. The parent who gave you cake knew it would make you happy. Once you become addicted, they have a lever they can control you with. "If you don't behave, you *won't* get dessert," or, "If you do behave, you *will* get a cookie."

Looking back at my childhood, it was all about getting that sugar fix in one way or another. Sure I'd have fun at the beach or swimming at the pool, but I *lived* for the ice cream sandwich I'd get after swimming or the frozen Milky Way I'd get right after arriving at the beach.

At school, there was chocolate milk, ice cream, and cookies. There was even a general store in town that sold candy in bulk. Almost every student would stop by at lunch to load up on gummy bears, Jolly Ranchers, Ring Pops, Jaw Breakers, M & Ms, Twizzlers, Nerds, and an endless supply of bubble gum and chocolate to help get them through the rest of their day.

I'd end up with so much candy on Halloween that it allowed me to stock up until the holidays, which led to more and more candy. In fact, all holidays seemed to be nothing more than excuses to consume sugar.

Summer trips to the New Jersey boardwalks included cotton candy, caramel apples, and saltwater taffy.

Whenever my mom baked a cake, she'd let me lick the spatula and the bowl she mixed it in, which contained a fair amount of batter to begin with.

After school we always hit 7-11, supplying us with unlimited quantities of Big Gulps, Slurpees, donuts, cookies, ice cream, and candy.

Breakfast not only included pancakes drenched in maple syrup, but lots of high sugar cereals like Lucky Charms, Applejacks, and Trix. If I had Wheaties or Raisin Bran, I'd add my own sugar, and a LOT of it.

Fast food restaurants had ice cream sundaes and milkshakes. Regular restaurants had multiple dessert options including pies, cakes, and mousses. I'd have soda most of the time with my meal but when I was very young I remember drinking a lot of Shirley Temples, which is ginger ale and grenadine, a red, sugary substance containing high fructose corn syrup, among many other undesirable ingredients.

I couldn't chew enough bubble gum as a kid. Some of my favorite brands were Big League Chew, Bazooka, Bubblicious, Hubba Bubba, and Bubble Yum (providing it wasn't sugarless)! Even the baseball cards I collected as a kid came with gum.

I found myself popping chewable Fred Flinstone vitamins behind my mom's back because they were loaded with sugar. The same with Aspergum, cough drops, and chewable baby aspirin.

Finally, you had our family freezer, stuffed with all kinds of frozen desserts and ice cream, which everyone loves, and for good reason. They're loaded with sugar, fat, and sodium, which are the most addictive foods you can consume. Not to mention all the addictive chemicals thrown in for good measure.

My point of this extensive trip down memory lane is that the children of today are no different than I was. They are getting their sugar fix on all day everyday, and they will stop at nothing to get it. When kids eat sugar, they are louder, ruder, wilder, crazier, and bouncing off walls with hyperactivity because their brain chemistry is now completely unstable. The number of children around the world on psychiatric medicine today is off the charts. It's very hard to keep a focused thought when you have toxic poison running through your veins all day!

As far as I'm concerned, sugar is the real gateway drug. In my case, it also led to a mouth full of cavities at a very young age. By the time my 30's rolled around I finally woke up and steered away from most candy, soda, and sweets, but continued getting my fix from alcohol, fruit juice, and complex carbohydrates like pasta, bread, and potatoes, all of which are converted to sugar in the bloodstream within 30 minutes of consumption.

Sugar not only feeds human cells in the form of proper glucose, it also feeds viruses, bacteria, mold, fungus, yeast, etc. In fact, all sugars that go beyond what the human cell can ingest, burn, and utilize have the potential to feed every known disease. Additionally, non-digested sugar converts to fat, so when a person is overweight, the chance for every known disease goes up.

Unless you're extremely athletic, your body only needs about 2 teaspoons of glucose, or 8 grams of sugar, per day. This amount can be obtained from eating 2 small salads. One can of soda has 40 grams of sugar. The average person eats about 150 pounds of sugar every year, or about a half a cup per day.

In the US alone, there are over 100 million cases of diabetes or low blood sugar, almost a third of the population. Pharmaceutical companies now have separate buildings just to create insulin in.

Sugar has the ability to suppress the immune system, cause hypoglycemia and obesity, interfere with the absorption of vitamins and minerals, and contributes to the creation of cancer and many multitudes of other diseases.

90 percent of grocery store foods have sugar in them in one form or another. Reading food labels is a necessity. There are tons of words for sugar but ultimately they all have the same effect on the body. Most words end in OSE, like fructose, sucrose, dextrose, etc. However, it is just as bad to use honey, agave, maple syrup, barley malt, etc. Additionally, the sugar substitutes like aspartame, saccharine, and Xylitol are loaded with chemicals and things you really don't need if your desire is to obtain optimum health.

The only exception is stevia, which is a natural sweetener and sugar substitute made from the leaves of the plant species stevia rebaudiana. It does not have the same effect on the body and blood sugar and is one of the positive addictions I used to rid sugar from my diet. It's a safe alternative because the digestible protein in the herb magnetizes and takes sugar out of the bloodstream, so it actually helps regulate blood sugar as opposed to spiking it.

Organic stevia extract is the best option for consumption.

Once you've licked refined sugar and all it's alternatives, be aware that the second way to get sugar is by eating massive amounts of bread, potatoes, pasta or other complex carbohydrates. As I mentioned, these foods break down into sugar in the bloodstream within 30 minutes. Moderation is ok, but the constant consumption is what you want to avoid out of respect to your pancreas. The pancreas regulates sugar and by overloading it, you're doing potential short and long term damage.

This is why you need to be cautious of the third way to get sugar, fruit, as well. The fiber in fruit helps to slow the uptake absorption of sugar, so it's better to eat whole fruit rather than drink its juices. Fruit juice has not only been pasteurized, making it void of nutrients, it has as much or more sugar than soda. And while I say eating whole fruit is better, it too must be done in moderation; otherwise you're up against the fructose factor again.

Another concern with fruit is that it has been hybridized over the years to be sweeter and sweeter. It is estimated that the fruit we eat today is 30 times sweeter than the fruit our ancestors consumed. Even worse is that fruit, when picked unripe, robs the body of nutrients, takes enamel off the teeth, causes cavities, erodes bone marrow, and takes the sheathing off the nerves. It's highly acid, and acts like a sponge. Because it doesn't have a full nutrient spectrum, it takes what it needs from your body. And unfortunately, most fruit you get at markets, even organic, is picked unripe, so it is less likely to spoil during shipping and will have a longer shelf life. What this boils down to is that unless you have a fruit tree and let it drop naturally off the vine, you're getting unripe fruit.

A YouTube video I highly recommend is "Sugar, the Bitter Truth,'" by Dr. Robert Lustig. Dr. Lustig not only points out the harmful affect that sugar has on the body, but the alarmingly negative affect that fruit sugar, or fructose, has on the body as well. The way it is processed by the human body is almost identical to the way the body processes ethanol. In fact, he literally refers to fructose as "ethanol without the buzz."

Personally, I gave up most fruit except lemons, which are low in sugar, and have an alkalizing affect on the body. I also eat some fruits that are not usually considered fruits, like avocados, tomatoes, cucumbers, and olives. But again, these are all extremely low in sugar and can be eaten in moderation without concern. I also consume berries occasionally, which for the most part are also low in sugar, extremely alkalizing, and chock full of antioxidants and phytochemicals. However, if I can't find organic varieties of any of the above, I don't consume them at all.

If you do eat fruit, I wouldn't recommend your diet consisting of more than 15 percent of it. Ideally, fruit should also be eaten on an empty stomach, as it doesn't mix well digestively with proteins and starches. It especially does not mix with grains, because the end result of sugar mixed with grain is of course, alcohol! Yet this is a fact that goes over the collective head of most people.

A good suggestion is to taint a glass of water with fruit juice so that it's 90 percent water, and 10 percent juice. I did this when getting off fruit juice myself, and found it to be very valuable.

The amino acid Glutamine not only fends off cravings for alcohol, but sugar too, and was definitely helpful in fending off mine.

Obviously, this chapter is not going to win me any popularity contests, but that's ok. The clarity of consciousness I've experienced since getting off sugar has been worth its weight in gold and I believe one day in the future, this substance will be looked at the same way cigarettes are today.

The bottom line is that the sugar industry is not going away anytime soon. The only option you have comes from individual choice. All I ask is to consider going without it for 3 months so you can see if you feel better or worse, and determine if you're addicted. Be careful of excuses like, "This doesn't have much sugar in it," or, "I'll just have one bite." Zero sugar means ZERO sugar. I'm not saying it's easy to do, but that validates my point all the more. The reason sugar is in everything is because it's an addictive drug that sells, and almost all of us are addicted to it in one form or another.

If you do go down the sugarless path, remember again that it takes time to incorporate these changes into your life. Even with positive addictions in line to replace the negative ones, be realistic. You can't make up for 40 years of abuse in 1 or 2 years. It's a lifestyle change that must be done gradually. Understand that the more time goes by, the better you will feel. Additionally, the less sugar you ingest, the less you'll ultimately want to consume.

5 CONSUMPTION 101

The next destructive vice I had to eliminate was processed food, because it is loaded with chemicals, preservatives, artificial ingredients, and usually contains high amounts of sugar, fat, and sodium to boot. This was tough because processed food is EVERYWHERE and I'd been eating it my entire life, but if I were to ever regain my health and feel better, I knew it had to be eliminated or majorly scaled back from my diet.

Refined foods have been stripped of their fiber, vitamins, minerals, antioxidants, and micronutrients. They're simple carbohydrates like white flour, wheat flour, refined sugar, pastries, white pasta, white bread, white rice, french fries, cupcakes, cookies, crackers, soft drinks, and similar junk foods. Pretty much everything my diet consisted of when I started down this path, except you'd have to add in a ton of meat, dairy, fat, grease, and alcohol!

When living with my mom, my breakfast was usually bacon, eggs, toast, and hash browns. Lunch was usually McDonald's or Burger King. As disgusting as this food is, the worst part is after you eat it, you're still hungry because it has no nutrients, so as far as your body thinks, it's starving. Therefore I'd have to eat an early dinner around 5 or 6pm. The amount of weed I was smoking didn't help either.

I was definitely not an easy person to live with during this period. My moods swings were terrible at best. If 2 or 3 hours went by without eating, I wouldn't get annoyed; I'd get livid. And dinner was the least healthy meal of the day. I insisted on cooking 95 percent of the time for my mother and I. I felt like it was the only small way I could give back, though the way I cooked, I wasn't doing either of us any favors, health wise. We had chicken, ham, turkey, pork chops, hamburgers, hot dogs, and steak on a nightly basis and it was usually fried in butter or oil. When we'd order in, we'd get deep dish, stuffed crust pizza, or something similarly high in calories. There was also an endless supply of snacks, chips, and desserts.

When cutting back on processed food, it's important to read labels, but if you eat real, whole food, there are no labels to read. That said;

a general rule is that the longer list of ingredients on the label, the less potential it has for health and nutrition.

Cooked and processed foods cause acidity in the body because they lack the oxygen and enzymes necessary for absorption. This allows undigested food to float around the bloodstream causing the potential for many health problems. Dr. Otto Warburg, who won a Nobel Prize for his work in 1931, concluded that oxygen deprivation was a major cause of cancer. Additionally, with a steady supply of oxygen to all cells, cancer could potentially be prevented indefinitely. Processed food has no oxygen, and even oxygen rich foods lose their oxygen content when cooked. Therefore, "living food" is the highest quality food you can eat, because all of the vitamins, minerals, amino acids, carbohydrates, oxygen, hormones, and enzymes are all intact.

Seeds are, in their embryonic state, a primary food containing the entire pattern of the atoms, molecules, cells, and tissues that will appear as its plant when it's fully-grown. If you cook or roast a seed and then plant it, it will not grow. It is dead food because you have killed the enzymes in it. Enzymes are extremely important for us to be in good health because they have a major role in building, cleansing, and healing the body, as well as being essential for good digestion. Because we are born with a limited supply at birth, we need to obtain back up from the food we eat. However, enzymes die when food is cooked at a temperature of 118 degrees or higher.

This is a huge part of the equation in my opinion. Scientists estimate that there are roughly 8.7 million species on the planet, yet humans are the *only* ones who cook and process food. Domesticated pets now are a part of that club and have therefore seen a steady decline in their health as well. All other species eat food in its natural, unprocessed state, but humans actually go out of their way to destroy the nutritional value of their food before eating it. The bottom line is the greater your intake of cooked and processed food, the greater your risk is for ill health and disease.

Nutrients are vitamins, minerals, fats, carbohydrates, proteins, and amino acids that are frequently categorized as essential and nonessential. The first was discovered in the early 1900's but it has only been really since the 1950's that the roles of nutrients became associated with vitamins and minerals that work within the body as components to enzymes and hormones. Essentially, by cooking food at high temperatures, you are eliminating the nutrients right out of it.

One nutrient that used to be essential, but no longer is, is fiber. Fiber rich food could not be sold overseas because it would spoil rapidly. So the bulk of fiber was stripped away from our food more than a century ago. It is estimated that our ancestors ate 100 to 300 grams of fiber daily, where as now, the average person consumes less than 10 grams a day. Having enough fiber in your diet normalizes bowel movements, lowers cholesterol levels, regulates blood sugar, and aids in achieving healthy weight. There is virtually no fiber in junk food, processed food, and fried food.

Speaking of which, everyone seems to know fried food isn't good for you, but practically everything is fried at restaurants, and you're hardly ever getting organic. Sure it tastes good and it's extremely addictive, but along with it you also get all the chemicals, heavy metals, hormones, antibiotics, pesticides, and herbicides. Additionally, there is more empirical evidence that fried food creates disease than almost all other food. Linked to its consumption you will find everything from to clogging of the arteries to high cholesterol, high blood pressure, heart attacks, strokes and Alzheimer's. When you heat oil, lipid peroxidation occurs, which is carcinogenic. That's one reason I got off Omega 3 fish oil supplements. The other is because of all the toxins and heavy metals in fish. I know. I know...killjoy number 200 of *No More Mr. Vice Guy* and we're only on page 32!

The fact is almost everything is backwards

from the way it should be in life. But there's no money in that! Restaurants want you addicted to their food, so they use maximum amounts of fat, sugar, and salt to assure that becomes a reality.

When I started down this path, I had major brain fog, allergies, headaches, and hypoglycemia. Not just from sugar consumption, but also from all the preservatives, artificial colors, flavors, and chemicals I was consuming. As I write this, I haven't had a single headache in almost 3 years. My allergies, brain fog, and hypoglycemia cleared up too, and a lot of it has to do with the fact that I stopped eating processed food, which includes fried food at restaurants.

Ultimately, I still eat 25 percent of my food cooked. That's measured by weight, not volume. When I do cook, I keep the heat as low as possible, use glass cookware, and don't use oils.

Early on along my road to recovery, I stopped microwaving my food too. I've yet to find any positive research about the many benefits of zapping our food with radiation. Have you? We tend to want things NOW, and sometimes don't stop to consider the potential consequences.

Cutting out sugar, alcohol, caffeine, and processed food all fall into the category of a very simple principal that anyone can incorporate into their lifestyle. That is; *only eat things that have high nutritional value.* By doing that you are automatically eating low calorie, as the highest quality foods we can eat are measured by the amount of nutrients they have, not by caloric value. Therefore, a calorie is not a calorie, as so many people mistakenly believe including me before I started doing research for this book!

As for the positive addiction I used to replace processed and refined food, I simply chose to incorporate a lot of raw, organic, living food into my diet. The more of it I got into my body as time went on, the better I felt mentally, physically, emotionally, and spiritually.

6 FOR THE LOVE OF ANIMALS

So now I'd given up or scaled WAY back on alcohol, sugar, caffeine, & processed food, as well as incorporated a lot of fresh raw food into my diet. The next thing that had to go was meat and dairy.

Wait a minute. Did I just say that? Admittedly, I *never* thought I'd even consider the concept of cutting out meat or dairy, but my research led me to realize that perhaps I'd been brainwashed by certain multi billion industries into thinking it was something I needed to be healthy.

Like caffeine and sugar, how would I ever know what it felt like to *not* eat meat and dairy unless I gave it a try? It was not my intention to become a vegan at the start of this journey. It was my intention to feel better as a human being and achieve clarity of consciousness; that's all.

I was always an animal lover, so technically, it weighed on my conscience from time to time, but I really never gave it much thought, because "everyone" did it, and we are brought up believing we need meat to get protein and build muscles and milk to get calcium and build strong bones or we'll fall apart.

After eating meat and dairy on a daily basis for almost 40 years, you can imagine my surprise when I started to actually do some research on my own and came to the conclusion that there is overwhelming biological evidence to support that humans are actually herbivorous beings.

Legitimate, meat-eating carnivores have a digestive system that has 20 times more stomach acid. They have claws and fangs made for tearing flesh and their jaw joints have an up and down vertical hinge. Herbivores have sliding jaw joints and grinding back molars that allow them to chew in a rotary motion to grind grains and greens. Carnivorous animals have colons that are constructed for quick elimination. The bowel of humans is a long and windy path full of sharp turns, making it very difficult for meat of any kind to easily pass through.

That's just the biological logic. What about health concerns?

Most meat is riddled with herbicides, fungicides, pesticides, and other chemicals that are sprayed directly on the food the animals consume. They are also pumped full of hormones, antibiotics, growth stimulants, and all sorts of drugs to fatten them up and keep them from dying from the extremely unhealthy conditions they live in.

It's also important to consider the adrenaline factor. If you had a choke chain around your neck to keep you in line on a moving conveyer belt, while all those in front of you were being beheaded, chances are you'd have a fair bit of adrenaline running through your veins at the time of your death. Unused adrenaline is extremely toxic and it is packed into all meat, whether the animal is slaughtered "humanely" or not.

Meat is also a major source of uric acid, cholesterol, and saturated fat, all known to be harmful to human health. It also has *zero* grams of fiber in it.

The China Study, written by Dr. T. Colin Campbell has sold well over a million copies since it was first published in 2005, and is based on the most comprehensive study of nutrition ever conducted. Tracking 6500 adults in China over a 20-year period, it compares those on predominantly plant-based diets with those who consumed meat and dairy regularly. The bottom line is that all animal foods were responsible or linked to all major diseases, and those who eliminated animal products from their diets achieved better much better health and longevity.

Much of the research deals with casein, the primary protein component in cow's milk. Tumor growth could literally be turned on and off by the consumption of casein, which is also used as an adhesive to make glue. Imagine what it does to our insides!

At some point I also had to logically ask myself the question if I thought we were really meant to suck milk out of any animal's breast aside from our own mother's at birth. Humans are the *only* creatures on earth that drink milk from another species. You'll never see a kangaroo suckling an alligator tit, or a chimpanzee drinking milk from a Billy Goat breast. Additionally, milk is one of the most mucus forming foods you can consume and is absolutely loaded with fat, cholesterol, hormones, antibiotics, pesticides, herbicides, and most disgusting of all, puss!

A growth hormone called or Insulin-like Growth Factor One or IGF − 1, is the ingredient in milk responsible for rapidly turning a 60-pound calf into a 600-pound cow. What do you think it does to the anatomy of poor, unsuspecting children?

And as for calcium, the only reason milk is good source is because cows eat a ton of green leaves. So, *why not cut out the middleman and just eat the green leaves direct?*

In 2011, Dr. Campbell, wrote the forward to a book called *Life Force*, written by the director of the Hippocrates Health Institute, Dr. Brian Clement. Hippocrates got its name from the father of modern medicine himself, who 2500 years ago said, "Let food be thy medicine and medicine be thy food." Brian and his wife, Anna Maria Clement, have been directing the institute since 1980, taking over for Ann Wigmore, who founded it in 1963. Wigmore, a well-known naturopath and alternative medicine advocate known for healing the natural way through a diet of raw, organic, living foods, healed herself of stage 4 colon cancer. At Hippocrates, no one is ever told they will be healed. Rather they are given the tools they need to rebuild their immune systems and mindset so that the body can heal itself. And a big part of the way they go about doing it is by eliminating meat and dairy from the diet.

Two of Brian's books, *Life Force*, along with *Living Food for Optimum Health*, are among the best I've read in the world of nutrition and are highly recommended for anyone wanting to get to the bottom line on health and longevity. He also runs a very informative website called www.therealtruthabouthealth.com and has recently authored a 3-volume book set for the academic community called *Food IS Medicine*, which references thousands of scientific studies affirming the fundamental role that unprocessed, unheated plant based food play in the process of disease recovery and prevention.

After reading *The China Study* and Brian Clement's books, the evidence that meat and dairy were absolutely not good to consume made complete sense. However, it wasn't really the research that convinced me to give them up. It was the way I felt. Meat and dairy are very acidic and are major contributors of clogged arteries due to their high saturated fat content. My father had an angioplasty done in 1995 and went to his grave with major arteries blocked in his legs and neck. I was fast on the way to creating the same conditions in my body, except I was doing it in half the time!

I decided to get rid of meat first. Initially, I cut out bacon in the morning, and scaled meat at dinner down to 3 nights a week vs. 7, eventually getting my consumption down to about once a week. And when I say meat, I mean any kind of decomposing flesh; fish, chicken, and turkey included. I started replacing the meat dishes with Tofu or Tempeh initially. Fake deli meats and vegan cheeses also did their jobs to get me started. But when I read the labels on these products, it was clear to me that I was not benefiting my health in any way by consuming them. They are highly processed, highly cooked, and contain many chemicals and preservatives. However, transitional or bridge foods are needed initially for each phase of a diet when you are trying to rid something from it. They are temporary, and your body will let you know how long to consume them for. While they are not exactly healthy, they're usually a much healthier choice than what you've been eating up to that point.

The healthier you get, the less bad food you desire. Even pasta. Even pizza. Two foods I didn't ever think it was possible to feel that way about. I'm not saying they aren't delicious. I'm saying that they are void of any significant nutritional value, and the more you eat foods that do have significant nutritional value, the more your own body instinctively begins to put it all together.

Now I know why for the first time in 40 years I actually feel satiated after I eat. My body is finally getting what it needs. I feel absolutely great and have tons of energy to get me through each day.

It wasn't until a year in that I graduated from vegetarian to vegan, and another 6 months went by before I arrived at the 75 percent raw vegan level I am at today. This was done purely by instinct. My body kept telling me what I needed throughout this entire journey and I'm forever grateful for the wisdom it has provided me.

It's also important to mention that initially; I did not feel so fantastic because my body was in the state of detoxifying. But once I got past that period, the real reward and benefits became extremely significant.

Equally important to consider is that since I went vegan, my bowel movements have been about 85-90 percent less offensive. People with pet rabbits know exactly what I'm talking about. Since rabbits are vegetarian, they can crap in their cage for weeks, and there's no need to clean it out because of odor concerns. Cats on the other hand are carnivores, and what comes out the back end of these animals smells so bad, even they know it must be buried immediately. Remember; you are what you eat!

7 PROTEIN POWER

The first questions I had about being vegan were, will I get enough protein and where will I get it from? After doing research, I logically concluded that if a vegan diet has enough protein for gorillas, elephants, horses, giraffes, buffalo, and rhino, it must have enough for humans.

How do these animals gain such massive muscle from eating grasses, plants, shrubs, and grains? Because all life on the planet comes from the sun, and all nutrients are captured on the leaf of a plant. So, the initial logic of the meat industry was to let the animal eat the plant; then we eat the animal and receive the protein. Again, *why not cut out the middleman and just eat the plants direct?*

A diet high in raw chlorophyll not only strengthens the immune system, but also delivers a continuous energy transfusion into the blood stream that is automatically high in digestible protein. Digestibility is a major factor and is often overlooked when determining how much protein one should consume. It turns out that *excess* protein is a primary cause of death by degenerative disease. Many forms of cancer as well as heart disease, diabetes, liver, and kidney dysfunction have all been linked to the overconsumption of animal protein. The human body doesn't have the necessary hydrochloric acid to break it down, as do carnivores like wolves, dogs, and cats. These animals have massive hydrochloric acid and a very small intestinal tract. Humans, on the other hand, have low amounts of hydrochloric acid and an elongated digestive tract, making meat next to impossible to digest. The average meat eater has 5 – 15 pounds of undigested meat in their colon at any given time.

Other sources of protein like nuts and seeds can be difficult to digest as well, but if you *soak and germinate* them first, you are giving life back to them, turning them back into plants that are ready to spawn trees with tens of thousands of nuts or seeds. Sprouting unlocks the ability to digest the protein so that it's available to the human body.

All protein is made up of amino acids. There are 9 essential amino acids we must obtain for optimum nutrition. When you germinate and sprout nuts and seeds, the condensed proteins become predigested and are considered "complete" proteins, because they contain all 9 essential amino acids your body needs. A few examples are Sunflower, Flax, and Sesame seeds.

Plant protein is not only high in amino acids; it's also highly digestible for humans. Blue green algae is 54 percent protein and has already been predigested and broken down into simple amino acids. Its close cousin, chlorella, is 52 percent protein, making these foods compact and extraordinary in their nutritional spectrum.

Comparatively, red meat is only 19 percent protein and the amino acids present in meat are almost all gone within 24 hours. In order to get a complete protein from an animal, you'd have to sever its head and drink the blood from its jugular vein almost immediately after it is slaughtered. Additionally, meat leaves residue behind like saturated fat and uric acid, clogging arteries, raising blood pressure, and leaving you susceptible to many health problems.

As far as eggs go for a protein source, my research shows that they are completely indigestible for human consumption. One egg has over 200 milligrams of cholesterol, of which our bodies needs exactly none. Additionally, eggs are really chicken fetuses, a fact that most people seem to be unaware of or in denial about.

It takes life to beget life. Life is dynamic, magnetic, and organic. Death is static, nonmagnetic, and inorganic.

Protein is the fiber of all life. It holds everything together. Without proper protein intake, the house you are building to store all the vitamins, minerals, essential fats and phytochemicals will have a faulty foundation. Having enough protein also regulates blood sugar. The anger and crankiness I felt so much after an hour or two of not eating went away on this diet because for the first time in my life I was getting enough *digestible* protein.

Three of the most critical foods to achieve good health are sprouts, sea vegetables, and freshwater algae. They contain the highest amount of solar energy in the most digestible form available. They also have the most protein in them by weight than any other foods you can consume.

Blue Green Algae was the very first life form on the planet, and has the exact same chemistry of essential fatty acids as the human brain. Fish are excellent sources of essential fats because they eat algae. Then we eat the fish, and gain the benefits from the essential fats. Once more, *why not cut out the middleman and just eat the algae direct?* There is so much toxicity in fish and fish oil to me it's an absolute no brainer to avoid it. The smell alone has put me off since my earliest childhood. Additionally, heated oil of any kind becomes a lipid peroxide, which is a well known carcinogen. The purest Blue Green Algae comes from Klamath Lake, Oregon and is manufactured by a company called E3 Live, and can be found in most reputable health food stores. It comes in frozen or powdered form.

High amounts of healthy omega 3 can also be obtained from germinated nuts and sprouted seeds like flax, chia, walnuts, and hemp, while sunflower, pumpkin, and watermelon seeds are all complete proteins and high in omega 6.

Sea vegetables like Kelp, Dulse, Nori, Irish Moss, & Wakame are excellent source of essential fats, protein, vitamins, and minerals. When I initially incorporated them into my diet, my satiation went up an entire level. I use them on salads, but if you don't like the taste you can always get them in supplement form too.

Fermented, raw, rice protein is an excellent source for protein powder, as well as hemp, peas, and other plant based sources. The ones to watch out for are soy, because it's been hybridized a lot over the years and is difficult to digest, and whey protein, which is a waste product from the dairy industry and should not be consumed at all.

Bee pollen is also an excellent source of protein. It is one of nature's most complete and nourishing foods because of its full spectrum of nutrients, amino acids, and enzyme content. It's also super concentrated, so it only takes small amounts to obtain one of the best natural multivitamins available.

Pollen also has an extremely wide array of digestive enzymes, which help break food down into usable nutrition, enabling us to get more out of what we eat, and therefore making us feel more nutritionally satisfied. It's also a good source of lecithin, which helps break down fats so we can assimilate them properly.

Bee Pollen also inhibits the release of histamine, which makes it helpful for seasonal allergies and hay fever. In fact, mine went away completely after I'd been taking it for only a few weeks! This is thanks to an antioxidant called Rutin, along with the theory of desensitization, where the pollen granules are thought to contain the allergen and will build up resistance, causing the production of antibodies when exposure occurs. Therefore, local sources are always best for treating seasonal allergy symptoms. It's good to start with only a few granules to make sure you're not allergic, and then work your way up to 2 or 3 tablespoons a day.

The meat and dairy industries are going to keep doing what they've been doing, so once again, the only choice we've ever had is to wake up on an individual level. One person at a time, we *can* make a difference. The evidence is there for anyone who wants to discover it.

Some books that were extremely eye opening and excellent reads on the vegan world are *Diet For a New America* by John Robbins, Gabriel Cousen's *Creating Peace by Being Peace,* and *Eating Animals* by Jonathan Safran Foer.

There are also some very informative documentaries like "Earthlings," "Food Inc." or "Vegucated." If you have the stomach to watch them, they will take you on a slaughterhouse tour so you can see first hand how these so called "foods" are prepared. We walk into a supermarket and all the meat is already been dead for months. And because it is essentially dead food void of nutrients, what is the point of eating it anyway? For most people like it was for me, it's nothing more than a destructive vice they've been addicted to for their entire lives.

Now, do I go around trying to convert others to lead a vegan lifestyle? No, because any time you are crusading in the name of peace, you're still vibrating a lot of resistance. I believe the secret to living the healthiest and happiest life comes from giving up resistance on all levels. You can offer wisdom to others, but unless they are ready to change, it's pointless to try and convince them of anything.

Remember; 3 short years ago, I thought the entire concept of a vegan lifestyle was downright insane, along with anyone who followed it. However, by staying open minded and skeptical,

I found that once again, the Universe is unpredictable when it comes to the manifestation of strong desires, even unconscious ones.

In the end, it's about loving yourself unconditionally. Once you are able to do that, you will be able to love others unconditionally as well. You will accept them without trying to change them and understand that every person that comes into our lives is doing the absolute best they can do, based on their present level of awareness. That's all the universe will ever allow.

8 SPROUTAHOLIC

So, nutritionally speaking, if plant based food was where the action was, my goal was to figure out which had the most nutrients, and after extensive research, the answer was abundantly clear; sprouts!

Full of vitamins, minerals, and complete proteins, sprouts are just about the best food you can eat. They are biogenic living plant foods, meaning they transfer their life energy to you. Sprouts, along with geminated nuts, seeds, grains, and legumes, are alkalizing, life generating, revitalizing, high-energy foods that are high in enzymes and predigested complete proteins.

By sprouting and germinating nuts, seeds, grains, and legumes, the nutrient content skyrockets, and the food becomes ten to thirty times more nutritious than the most nutritious organic vegetable you can grow outside in your garden. That's not 10 to 30 percent; it's 10 to 30 *times* more nutritious. Sprouting beans is the ideal way to eat them, as they will be much easier to digest and not produce the intestinal gas they do when cooked. As for grains, sprouting them depletes the entire gluten factor, and makes them far more alkalizing as well.

If your goal is to get the most amount of nutrition for the least amount of calories, it doesn't get much better than sprouts. While they are available in health food stores and supermarkets, growing your own ensures absolute freshness and maximum living energy. And it's a whole lot cheaper. One pound of seeds will yield about 10 pounds of sprouts. I buy my non-gmo, organic seeds in bulk, and then sprout them in my kitchen using mason jars. I've been sprouting for almost 3 years now, and it makes up about 60 percent of everything I eat. The money I've saved is a nice perk, but the real benefit is getting the additional nutrition and energy that these baby plants provide.

The staple sprouts in my diet are clover, broccoli, radish, alfalfa, mustard, and fenugreek. I also sprout legumes like Mung beans, red, green, and black lentils, adzuki beans, navy beans, chickpeas, fava beans, and whole green peas. Pound for pound, lentils and other bean sprouts contain as much protein as red meat, yet they are totally digestible and contain none of the fat, cholesterol, hormones, or antibiotics found in most meat. In the nut and seed family, I sprout Brazil nuts, walnuts, sunflowers seeds, flax seeds, chia seeds, pumpkin seeds, watermelon seeds, almonds, and sesame seeds. In the grain family, I sprout amaranth, millet, oats, barley, quinoa, wheat, rye, kamut, spelt, and teff.

By sprouting, not only are the enzyme inhibitors removed, but, as previously mentioned, the gluten factor also becomes null and void. It turns normally acidifying foods like beans and grains into much healthier, alkalizing alternatives.

Being a bachelor makes this lifestyle a bit easier for me, but anyone can do it if they are serious about obtaining optimum health. It takes less than 5 minutes a day. If your lifestyle is too busy or if you travel often, you can buy automatic sprouting machines that do all the work for you. A great website I recommend on sprouting is http://www.Sproutman.com; run by the sproutman himself, Steve Meyerowitz. There you can also find many tutorials, videos, sprouting tools, and even seeds. There are many reputable on-line seed companies that sell non-gmo, organic seeds for sprouting, but they can also be found occasionally at local grocery stores and farmer's markets.

Entire books have been written about sprouting methods, and there are countless instructional videos online that will provide you with all the help you need. But just to give you an idea of how easy it is, I use wide mouth mason jars, a cheesecloth like fabric for straining, and a rubber band to seal it around the top of the jar. I soak 2 to 4 tablespoons of seeds in distilled or purified water overnight, and drain them in the morning upon waking. I use a dish drainer to hold the jar at an upside down angle as they drain and dry, and continue rinsing them twice a day until they are fully-grown. Beans, nuts, and grains take about 2 days; while the seeds like alfalfa, clover, broccoli, and fenugreek take about 5. That's really all there is to it!

Personally, I find all sprouts delicious and eat them alone as a snack very often. However, they can also be added to main dishes, casseroles, soups, sandwiches, and salads.

Also considered sprouts are the tray grown grasses like wheatgrass, kamut, spelt, barley, buckwheat, sunflower, and pea greens. To grow these at home require trays, organic soil, lots of watering, and usually take about a week to ten days. I consider this too much of an effort for now, so I purchase mine in bulk at a local organic farm in San Diego.

After consuming meat for almost 40 years, I can honestly say that eating food that was alive felt like a vacation. Over a period of several weeks, I scaled my meat intake down to one night a week, and then moved off of it completely in January of 2013.

Since then I've had meat on a handful of occasions and literally became ill after ingesting it every time. The purer your body becomes, the less destructive vices it desires. Therefore, if you do go back to old habits, you'll feel the sting of their detrimental effects a lot more dramatically.

9 THE LIVING FOOD LIFESTYLE

In this chapter, I'll outline what I eat every day. Remember, this is not going to work for everyone because of individual body chemistries and allergic reactions to certain foods. Also, people choose their foods and pleasures according to their states of consciousness. Those who haven't yet snapped out of the brainwashing done by the industries mentioned in this book will most likely think I'm the one who's bonkers and I'm perfectly fine with that. All I can do is report the dietary choices that worked for me.

As previously mentioned, I start my day with 2 tablespoons of Bragg's Apple Cider Vinegar in a large glass of distilled water. Then I'll have a cup of organic tea of some kind, followed by another huge glass of distilled water.

I then take my chlorella supplements down with a nice glass of Blue Green Algae, and have found that 2 or 3 hours have usually passed by this time.

Then it's time to make 3 large Super Salads, which will make up the majority of food I'll eat for the day. As I plate my breakfast salad, I also prepare the other 2 in glass containers for lunch and dinner.

For the record, all food mentioned in this chapter is organic.

I start off by putting some spices on the plate like cayenne pepper, turmeric, and ginger.

Then I'll lay down a bed of greens as a base. I usually use a combination of dandelion greens, spinach, kale, and collards.

Following that I'll add several layers of sprouted beans like Mung, adzuki, navy, and lentils.

I then toss in multitudes of sprouts in the form of clover, broccoli, radish, fenugreek, and alfalfa.

Next up, I'll add some fresh, alkalizing herbs like basil, rosemary, sage, spearmint, cilantro, parsley, and dill. They have plenty of medicinal benefits and add a *ton* of flavor into the mix as well.

Then I'll spike the salad up with sea vegetables like Dulse & Kelp for their added mineral benefits.

After adding red and green onions to the mix, I throw in watercress, sunflower greens, celery, bok choy, cucumbers, asparagus, cabbage, and avacado.

Lastly, I mix in a variety of, sprouted, alkalizing grains like kamut, rye, barley, amaranth, quinoa, spelt and teff.

After tossing it several times, I top it off with a heaping tablespoon of bee pollen.

The 3 raw Super Salads I eat are in addition to the other food I consume at each meal. For example, along with my breakfast salad, I eat a big bowl of organic, sprouted, oatmeal. It's 95 percent raw. I lightly cook the other 5 percent to add a little warmth into the mix. To give it some flavor and spice, I add cayenne pepper, Ceylon cinnamon, a tablespoon of olive oil, a splash of lemon juice, and a pinch of sea salt.

For lunch, along with my Super Salad, I'll usually have an organic, flourless, sprouted whole grain muffin with either some brown rice or organic red potatoes. Other times I may have some kind of fake meat product, providing it is of the non-gmo variety, along with the sprouted muffin, or some baked organic tortilla chips. Occasionally, I'll lightly cook some sprouted beans and grains together and mix them in with tempeh or tofu.

As a snack between meals, I will usually eat some raw, sprouted nuts like almonds, Brazil nuts, flax seeds, sunflower seeds, or walnuts.

For dinner, I'll have my Super Salad along

with clear noodle pasta made from Mung beans. I still have traditional pasta occasionally, but try to avoid large quantities of it, and will usually eat sprouted, whole grain pasta as my first option if I can find it.

That's pretty much the food I consume on a regular basis for close to 3 years now. There's really no need to vary it up much because each salad has so much variation and nutrition packed into it already.

Occasionally however, I'll leave out the beans and grains and add nuts and seeds to the salad instead. For proper digestion, you don't want to combine a protein like a nut with a carbohydrate like a bean or grain. I did this in the beginning and suffered big time gas as a result. However, when I combined the food properly, I had no digestive issues at all.

For the dressing, I use Bragg's Liquid Aminos, Lemon Juice, and a tablespoon or two of extra virgin, cold pressed, organic olive oil.

The beauty of the *No More Mr. Vice Guy* diet is that there are no restrictions. If I desire a hamburger or a slice of pizza, I'll have it. The amazing thing is that, for the most part, I have no desire to consume those foods anymore. If I do, my body pays the price and I feel it in every orifice of my existence.

When you actually get healthy again, your body will naturally gravitate toward the healthiest options. It takes time, but after you've lost the weight and seen the positive changes in your life, you'll want to stick to the plan all the more.

Each person reading this will have to make their own variations to arrive at the ultimate diet and lifestyle choices that will work best for them. If you want to use mine as a general guideline, be my guest. I've definitely had tremendous results with it!

The best advice I can give is to begin looking at food as fuel. Become a person who eats to live as opposed to one who lives to eat, and you will be well on your way to achieving optimum health and transforming your life for the better.

10 ADDITIONAL ESSENTIALS

In 2009, Brian Clement wrote an excellent book called *Supplements Exposed,* exposing a harsh truth that approximately 92 percent of supplements on the market today are made synthetically in a laboratory by the Pharmaceutical Industry. And they are made out of made out of things like petrochemicals, oils and coal tars and turpentine. Like anything else, it's all about money and marketing.

Today, we need supplementation more than ever. But we have to avoid the harmful majority and obtain supplements are 100 percent, whole food, plant based. By eating a diet that is well-rounded, whole food and plant-based, you're already getting a lot of the nutrients. Supplementation assures that we get certain elements and nutrients that you no longer find in these plant-based foods that are often grown in depleted soil.

The only supplements I currently take are E3 Live Blue Green Algae, chlorella, and a bacteria based form of B12. If my cravings do go up for sugar or alcohol, I'll take Glutamine and GABA for a while again until they pass. However, that hasn't happened for over 2 years now.

As for Vitamin D, I get that from natural sunlight. There is nothing better for strengthening the immune system, and it's a shame that more people aren't outside enjoying the benefits. As I mentioned, all life on the planet comes from the sun, so it's important to get outside everyday and pay some respect. I like to catch some off peak hour rays while exercising, which is what the next chapter is all about.

Before we go there however, let's talk about water. Of course, pure water is essential to our health and well-being. In fact, next to oxygen, it is the most vital factor to our survival. It makes up 83 percent of your blood, 75 percent of your brain and muscles, helps your body absorb nutrients, regulates body temperature, removes waste, and helps convert food into energy.

However, most tap water includes chemicals like chlorine, fluoride, aluminum, copper, pharmaceutical drugs, and many other unwanted elements. This has an acidic effect on the body and it has even been reported that bottled water is no better when its PH levels are tested. One way to go is to purchase a reverse osmosis that takes most of the chemicals out the water and makes it alkaline. You can also make your own alkaline water by using distilled water and squeezing fresh lemon juice into it. Other methods call for baking soda or hydrogen peroxide.

The bottom line though, is that you won't need to drink as much water if you eat a lot of alkaline foods that are made up of natural distilled water, like organic fruits and vegetables. Water that comes from raw, organically grown fruits and vegetables is the best life giving water because it has been infused with solar energy, vitamins, organic minerals, and enzymes.

Enzymes can help you build up a natural resistance to any ailment as they help flush out the accumulated deposits of inorganic minerals and work to dissolve toxins that are buried deep in your tissues and organs.

The true secret of health lies in internal cleanliness. To be 100 percent healthy, a body must be free from deposits of inorganic minerals that come from city tap water and water from lakes, rivers, wells, and streams.

Distilled water has been turned into vapor so that its impurities are left behind. Upon condensing, it literally becomes pure water, free of all pharmaceutical drugs, plastics, chemicals and heavy metals. Distilled water is also the water that the human body is made up of.

It is for these reasons that I believe distilled water it the best choice for human consumption. Sir Jason Winters, who cured himself of terminal cancer, drank it exclusively and also believed it to be the best choice. Dr. Theodore Baroody, author of the excellent book, *Alkalize or Die*, is also a huge advocate, along with legendary health gurus Paul Bragg, Norman Walker, Jack LaLanne, and of course, Brian Clement.

There is misinformation on the Internet that distilled water leaches minerals out of the body. What it actually does is collect and remove toxic *inorganic* minerals. That's a huge difference and unfortunately, a big misunderstanding.

If you want to avoid the BPA factor and lugging home several gallons at a time from the supermarket, you can buy a distiller and make it yourself at home. They usually start off in the $200 range.

I think juicing organic fruits and vegetables is a good idea providing you have a proper juicer, but make sure the fruit is juiced in moderation, or the fructose factor will be ready to wreak havoc on you once again.

I'm not a big fan of blending because when you blend a food, not only are you destroying the majority of nutrients, you are oxidizing it by blowing air through it. Smoothies can be used for transitional purposes, but by and large, they are not nutritious to consume. Because they aren't chewed, blended foods ferment in the stomach, making them very difficult to digest. This is why so many smoothie advocates are overweight or emaciated in my opinion.

Digestion starts in the mouth. The best juicers are your teeth. I can't overestimate the importance of chewing your food thoroughly and activating the digestive enzymes in your saliva. Processed food breaks down so easy in the mouth that we barely have to chew it. If I didn't take my time and thoroughly chew the 3 Super Salads I eat everyday, I'd still be in a lot of trouble, digestively speaking. It's also important to floss after every meal when consuming raw food.

Remember that it's not just eating healthy; it's also thinking healthy and acting healthy. I use fluoride free toothpaste, aluminum free deodorant, and make sure all soap, shampoos, hair gels, and shaving creams are organic. Household cleaning supplies are also natural and chemical free. Ultimately, even our clothing should be made of natural, organic fibers, as opposed to synthetic, man made materials.

Other elements like getting outdoors, exercising, breathing properly, meditation, stretching, being creative, and sexually satisfied are equally important to consider and must be incorporated into your lifestyle if your desire is to achieve balance, peace, harmony, happiness, and ultimately, a higher level of consciousness altogether.

11 MINDSET AND MOTION

Without exercise and the proper mindset, you can take everything I've said so far and throw it out the window. You could eat 100 percent raw organic food and still suffer health problems if negativity is still dominating your mindset and awareness. The good news is, once you shift to a healthier lifestyle and diet, your mindset usually shifts too.

Exercise is single handedly the best positive addiction anyone can incorporate into their lives. The body loves movement and the more you move, the better you feel. Because of the times we're living in, less people than ever before are getting out to obtain fresh air and oxygen.

Exercise releases endorphins in the brain. They are the body's natural painkillers and are extremely important in the aid of depression. Exercise has many other benefits too, like better circulation of blood throughout the body. The more blood you circulate, the more oxygen is carried to each cell. Nutrients get absorbed at a greater rate when we circulate the blood stream, and toxins come out of the body much faster too.

And you don't have to spend a lot of money either. Walking is free and you can do it anywhere. I walk outside 30-45 minutes a day, 6 days a week. Just about every great idea I've ever had comes to me on those walks, because I'm in the present moment when I receive them. I also like walking because it's a non-strenuous, aerobic activity that helps you burn fat, as opposed to an anaerobic activity where muscle is also lost.

Also extremely beneficial are resistance exercises like push-ups, pull-ups, sit-ups, and dips. You can pick up inexpensive weights at many thrift shops, and many public parks these days have built in exercise bars for working out as well. Many Yoga and Pilates classes are free or come with a very low cost. You can climb stairs if you live in an apartment building. The bottom line is there is no excuse not to get out there and move. Just get creative and have fun while you do it.

A huge key in my personal recovery was the discovery of Tai Chi and Chi Kung, and the incorporation of both into my exercise regime.

Chi Kung, the lesser known of the 2, is one of the most powerful forms of exercise ever, yet it almost involves no movement and a great deal of holding postures in certain positions. In fact, it can be done sitting! It only takes 15 to 30 minutes, builds and moves energy in the body, and with regular practice, has the ability to transform health in miraculous ways. It's also a great immune system builder and a great way to banish stress.

"Chi" is the Chinese term for energy, and "Kung" means exercise. It has been around for centuries, and is considered a very powerful form of meditation because it helps to calm and clear the mind. It will really give you an appreciation of energy like you've never had before. Life flourishes when there is an unobstructed flow of internal energy throughout the body. When that flow is blocked from stress or tension in our lives, it can easily putrefy. Practicing Chi Kung relieves this tension and clears those energy blockages.

Tai Chi is another natural way to build health and strength throughout the body, and can be very beneficial regardless of where one is along the path to recovery. It relaxes the mind, but also builds strength, flexibility, and stamina in the muscles and joints of your upper and lower body. Not exhausting or stressful in any way, it consists of a series of slow, continuous movements designed to develop and relax the entire body, building up the internal strength, suppleness, and stamina.

If you decide to go down either of these paths, I highly recommend 2 excellent books written by Master Lam Kam-Chuen. One is called *Step by Step Tai Chi*, and the other is *Everyday Chi Kung*.

Tai Chi and Chi Kung evolved out of meditation sessions I originally used to get off the majority of my vices. I'd usually sit and meditate in the sun for 30 to 45 minutes every day. It wasn't until about 6 months in that I incorporated movement in. I am a multi-tasker, after all.

I do a combination of aerobic, stretching, and weightlifting exercises 5 or 6 days a week minimally. I also do resistance exercises like push-ups, pull-ups, sit-ups, and dips. As a writer I sit a lot, so it's extra important for me to keep the wheels in motion to balance out the atrophy that would occur if I didn't. Lifting weights not only builds muscle and strength throughout the body, it enhances the continual development of hormones as well.

Speaking of keeping the wheels in motion, what about sex? I believe sexual energy is a universal fuel of life that nourishes mind, body, and spirit, and that remaining sexually active is one of the most effective ways to enhance your health and general well being. Therefore, I don't consider sex to be a vice in any way. Many of the foods I now consume are also natural, nourishing, aphrodisiacal ones that enhance the libido as well. Of course, sex can be highly addictive and can lead to problems for some people if they become consumed with it and let it take over their lives. I was definitely guilty of this in my 20's; the same decade I drank every night. Go figure! But in the end, I learned that the key was to enjoy sex in moderation...

Ok, maybe a little more than moderate is cool in this case. Like I said, exercise is single handedly the best positive addiction anyone can incorporate into their lives!

12 TRANSYLVANIA

For many years, I thought hypnosis had to do with being put under some kind of spell against your will, and from a distance it looked and smelled like complete bullshit. However, I came to the conclusion that all of us are hypnotized every day, in everything we do. The only question is, do you let the media and others decide it for you, or are you in control of your own hypnotic state?

I haven't watched a newscast in 10 years, nor do I even have basic cable. I only have a TV because I won it in a sales contest at my job. I watch movies occasionally and spend plenty of time on YouTube, seeking out things that make me laugh or lift my spirits, or to educate myself about a certain subject. Of course, I'll read major headlines to stay informed, but I no longer let the media dictate my moods based on what is shown on the news.

It all boils down to being aware of your emotions. They provide a built in guidance system to let you know at all times if you are headed in the right direction or not. Feeling negative emotion means you're swimming against the tide, and away from the things you want. Positive emotion means you're heading in the right direction, and all you have to do is let the current take you down the river.

Therefore, it's essential to eliminate all things from your life that stir up negative emotion in the first place, including the news, certain movies or TV shows, or even certain people, for that matter. This may not be easy, but there are many benefits to getting out of your comfort zone. Don't be afraid of change. Not only a good thing, it's the natural way of the Universe. When you go with the flow of it, the things you want will show up even faster because you'll have less resistance in your vibration.

I believe that creativity is where the heart of happiness is, and that we are born to create, not to compete. All comparison leads to unhappiness in one form or another. Someone or something is lowered in value, so therefore it's a form of a judgment. What is the point of comparison? What benefits come out of it other than gratification from the ego?

Even after the ego is stroked it makes no sense. Say you compare yourself to someone and decide that you are more knowledgeable about something than they are. Even if it's true, it doesn't mean that you're more knowledgeable than that person in all other aspects of life. There are things that person knows about other topics that would absolutely trump your awareness in comparison, but that doesn't elevate them either. No one is better than anyone else because at the core of our being, regardless of our race, creed, or color, we are all one mind expressing ourselves individually to evolve and expand consciousness as a whole.

Another difficult, but essential step is to give up caring what people think about you. You have ZERO control over it, so why waste any life energy over it? Of all the things I've ever done in attempt to better myself as a human being, this principle has changed my life for the better more than any other. It is hands down the most liberating and freedom inducing thing anyone can do for themselves, though it is not easy, and I'm not sure you ever get it done. But you can improve little by little over time, and when you do, you'll realize what a waste of time it was in the first place. It's a form of worry, which is also a waste of time. Worrying takes you out of the present moment, and that's where all your power is. The bottom line is, when you stop caring what other people think, you'll find yourself with a lot of free time on your hands. You begin to care about what really matters to you, and about the well being of others. By letting them be the way they are, you are doing them a favor by not infringing on their free will. You are also no longer judging yourself for any reason. The only judgment there ever can be is love. *If love is all you have to give, all you have to give is love.*

One of the biggest reasons I wrote my first book was to prove to myself that I could walk the walk. If I really didn't care what people thought, I could write and release the truth about my past, and free myself from it in the process. Yes, I was depressed, excessive, egotistical, arrogant, alcoholic, overweight, bankrupt and all the rest. I pursued careers as a comedian, actor, writer, director, producer, and failed at every single one of them, or at least failed to make a living at any of them. But ultimately, I realized that those experiences were absolutely necessary for creating a much better me. It's only when you can love the past and let it go that the resistance disappears from your vibration.

Additionally, when you no longer care what people think, you no longer have a desperate need for approval. The majority of comedians still have that need, and in my case, it stemmed from needing to stroke my ego, because I was really insecure and immature. I got into comedy because I saw it as a "stepping-stone" to break into acting. Though that didn't happen, something much better did. I came down to earth and got over myself, and if it weren't for stand up comedy, I would have never started down the spiritual path I am still following to this day. It will always be my desire to make others laugh, but I no longer do it for the reasons I used to, and in the end, that feels a lot better to me.

We've all heard the expressions, "Everyday above ground is a gift," and "Live everyday as if it were your last," but many of us fail to live up to them on the being level.

Everyday *is* a holiday. Life *should* be a celebration. That's why holidays don't exist in my reality tunnel. Sure, I'll celebrate them, but I also celebrate every other day of the year, so my level of excitement remains at an even keel. Holidays are nothing more than trances that require you to spend money. While they give people a much-needed break from the daily grind, my argument is that they keep people from living in the present. Their Christmas countdown begins in October, and that implies that this person is giving up the concept of celebration in their lives for the next 90 days, until *that day* arrives, then they'll go back to being miserable until the next "holiday."

We don't need holidays for a reason to celebrate life. Everyday is a gift in this physical reality and should be celebrated accordingly. The mood you are in on holidays can and should be the natural mood you are walking around in most of or all of the time.

A lot people are unaware that holidays are trances, so they can't wake up because they don't even know they're asleep. The same is true for people that thrive on negativity their whole lives, not even being consciously aware they are doing so. They spend their entire life de-evolving, and will continue to do so until their dying day. Thankfully, there are always positive options that allow us to evolve in the right direction when it comes to the choices we make on a daily basis.

It isn't easy to think clear when sugar, refined flour, caffeine, alcohol, drugs, and multitudes of other toxic chemicals are polluting your brain. Now that my clarity of consciousness has returned, I wouldn't exchange it for anything in the world. The beauty of it is, you can't have one without the other. Had I not de-evolved so far in the first place, I would never have evolved enough to write this book or master any of the principles in it.

It's not until we know what we really don't want in life that we know what we really do.

13 ALTERED STATES

Looking back at the vices I've shed, it's easy to see they are there own powerful forms of trances in and of themselves. The alcohol trance, the fast food trance, the sugar trance, the caffeine trance…what about the weed trance?

You've heard me mention a few times that my usage had grown out of control. Well, as you'll read, my new job required me to be 100 percent focused and sober in order to do it effectively, so I really didn't have a choice when it came to cutting back its usage. I still use medical marijuana in moderation, and believe it has many positive benefits as well. Therefore, like sex, it doesn't really qualify as your traditional vice.

Human beings have an innate ability to alter their states of mind, and I'm no different than anyone else. Hence the title of this book! We all have receptors in our brains that cause us to get high. Meaning, the drugs don't actually cause the high; they just help release the chemicals in our brains that are already there more efficiently. My ultimate desire is a find a way to release those chemicals naturally. As a big fan of altered states, I'm certainly willing to use myself as a guinea pig to see what works and what doesn't.

With alcohol, sugar, caffeine, processed foods, meat, and dairy, it was clear that they no longer worked for me and definitely needed to go. But with weed, there seems to be a level of brain circuitry and a connection to spirituality that I can't get to without ingesting it. I run into resistance when I think about quitting, so for now, it's best to make peace with it and do it in moderation.

As for going down the natural route, I did experiment with meditation for a period of time and had some very good results, but honestly, it can't hold a stick up to weed at press time. I also came to the conclusion that we did not come here to be put on pause. That's why I had better results with forms of "moving meditation" like Tai Chi and Chi Kung.

However, one form of meditation I will recommend is the use of a floatation tank, also known as a sensory deprivation tank. You float in a tank full of heated salt water, which is the same temperature as the surface of your skin.

Your eyes and ears are covered too. When our senses are taken away, it's easy to see that we are nothing but a blob of consciousness floating in a dark void. Therefore, *reality is nothing more than information*. Data. We each get our own individual data stream, which we interpret through our senses. Equally interesting to consider is that you cannot discuss "reality" without including yourself as part of the equation.

There are also many other potential benefits of floating, such as stress reduction, heightening and intensifying of all senses, and an increased ability to learn. My hope is that they eventually make their way into schools and universities. If children were brought up floating, it would give a whole new meaning to the definition of daydreaming, and they would probably shed their egos a lot faster as well.

It may not be for everyone, however. Some people hate being alone, and especially, alone with their own thoughts. For these types, floating may not be a good experience.

On the other hand, those who love who they are and enjoy being in the presence of their higher selves via yoga, mediation, or mind-altering substances, will most likely find it a paradise, and the closest possible way to experience the non-physical dimension while your body is still biologically alive.

14 LAUGH AND A HALF

The last trance I'd like to talk about is laughter. Humor has played a major role throughout my life. Since my earliest days of childhood, my father was making me laugh, either by being funny himself, or by introducing me to legendary comedians like George Carlin, Laurel & Hardy, Jackie Gleason, W.C. Fields, The Marx Brothers, and the Three Stooges.

Of course, humor is subjective. What I find funny, the next person may not, and vice versa. It's also everywhere, experienced by all ages and all cultures, making it truly universal.

It didn't take long for me to realize the reason I loved laughing so much was because of the way it made me feel, which is fantastic! Laughter is a reflex tool of our nervous system to release tension and restore a sense of well-being and relaxation. It takes your mind off any pain you may be experiencing prior to the onset. Even if you're not in pain, laughter decreases tension in muscles, while at the same time releasing endorphins in the brain, which are your body's natural painkillers. It enhances respiration, and provides exercise for muscles in the face, arms, legs, and stomach, as well as the diaphragm, thorax, circulatory and endocrine system.

Part of having a good sense of humor is being able to acquire a cosmic perspective of your own problems. Once you learn to laugh at yourself, it frees you up to laugh at others. Not so you can make fun of them, but because you can relate to them. The only people I let into my personal circle are ones that I consider to have a good sense of humor. My friends are people who not only I can make laugh, but who can make me laugh as well. I don't remember ever sleeping with a girl who didn't find me funny on some level. A sense of humor, if well executed, trumps any aphrodisiac available. I also take a genuine interest in the people I associate with, which allows me to relate to them in a humorous way, once I know what commonalities we share or what our differences may be.

Anger gets the best of us sometimes is because we fail to see any humor in the situation that has us fuming. It's hard to remember in that state of mind that we do have a choice when it comes to our reactions. Granted, it can be difficult to jump from pure hatred to a state of bliss just because you suddenly remembered you had a choice. But if you're willing to shift your perspective just a little, you'll be headed in a much better overall direction.

I feel blessed beyond my wildest dreams to be able to see life through the filter I do. My father had a very similar sense of humor, and in my opinion, it's the main reason we were so close. Humor forms a bond unlike any other. When we were together, you could count on funny things happening. Or perhaps because both of us found humor in just about anything and everything, it didn't matter what happened anyway.

And when it came to laughing at our own ignorance, nothing was funnier. The time we drove golf balls together was a perfect example. We rented our clubs and were told to get the balls outside. When we got out there, we found that a machine was responsible for the distribution. I put enough money in for 100 balls, but neglected to think about a basket for holding them, as did my father. As the balls came shooting out of the machine and everywhere around us, we both just stood there, Laurel and Hardy style, watching it all go down without once making any effort to capture or pick up any balls. The baskets turned out to be on the side of the machine and everyone looked at us like the real life Dumb and Dumber, but we didn't care. Not only did we laugh our asses off about it as we picked up all the balls, we laughed our ass off about it for the rest of my Dad's life. The memory itself became an inside joke, and I'm blessed to say it was one of hundreds.

Every book I've read about the healing power of humor includes a man named Norman Cousins, and how he overcame a terminal illness by laughing himself back to health. Around the clock, he did nothing but watch The Marx Brothers, Candid Camera, and any other programs that would make him laugh out loud. He wrote two books about his recovery, and though laughter was a key ingredient, he also took mega doses of Vitamin C, had a positive outlook on life, a lot of faith, hope, and love, and a hell of a will to live. It was a combination of all these things that led to his ultimate recovery, which no doubt came from his immune system being strong enough for him to heal himself.

Thanks to the Internet, we can now all do what Norman Cousins did, and experience as much comedy as we want on a daily basis. And this should go for the medical community too. I'm not suggesting doctors become comedians, or that laughter alone should replace current medical techniques. I'm saying the amount of money that would be needed to invest more humor into patients' lives is miniscule in comparison to what we are spending now on toxic chemicals to battle illness.

Humor was very beneficial to my father too. He lived 82 years in pretty good health without a sound diet or exercise of any kind. Love and laughter were dominant more than anything throughout his life, and as a result, most of the negative effects of his diet and lifestyle melted away like butter. He had many close friends with whom he shared laughs with, and a wife with whom he shared unconditional love and laughter with too. He enjoyed life to the fullest and basically lived to love and laugh. He taught me how to do so too, and for that, I am eternally grateful.

I realize if my Dad had been willing to clean up his lifestyle and dietary habits, he may be alive and well today. But ultimately, that's resistance. In the end, I learned to be thankful and appreciative for all of my father's influences, especially the negative ones, because they woke me up and led me to where I am today. Because of them, my time on the planet will likely be extended, as will anyone else's who reads this with an open mind that desires freedom from any vices. I've also learned valuable lessons I can pass on to my children. Therefore, my father's legacy will ultimately live on forever.

15 MANIFESTATIONS

While the journey of "de-vicing" myself has only been a few years in length, my spiritual journey actually started 15 years ago, in 2000. The most important lessons I've learned were discussed in my first book, but I'd like to reiterate a few here because they are so very important.

The first one is that our thoughts determine our realities, and we are all co-creators in them. We are all creating, all the time. Most people do it by default, but we all have the ability to become powerful deliberate creators. That's why I was harping so much earlier about clarity of consciousness. Without it, it's very easy to get off track, lose focus, and start thinking about and giving energy to the things we don't want, as opposed to the things we do.

If I had made all the changes I talked about in this book and kept a negative attitude, I'd still be in a lot of trouble. Happiness, peace, joy, love, and harmony are ours for the taking if we really want them. But to manifest them, we have to allow them to come into our lives, as opposed to resisting, which is what most people do most of the time.

The truth is, once we can relax and allow things to happen, the Universe will lead us without effort, to the right people, places, and circumstances to turn our dreams into reality, making us experts in the field of deliberate creation.

If you make peace with where you are, and take things one logical step at a time, you can absolutely manifest anything you want, and achieve any dream you've ever desired.

There are two methods of manifestation I recommend that I've had success with in the past.

Method # 1 is to make a step outline of everything that would need to transpire to make your goal a reality. Then take action on each step, crossing each one off as they are accomplished, and of course, remembering to enjoy the journey along the way as it all goes down. In my past, a take action plan was essential for things like producing a movie or writing a book. In both cases, I was initially intimidated by the size of my to-do list, but crossing off each step is a wonderful feeling, and when your ultimate goal or desire is about to manifest, it will no longer seem like such a daunting task, it will only seem like what it has become; the next logical step.

Method #2 is to write down or affirm what you want, have absolute faith it will become your reality, and completely detach yourself from the outcome. Trying to figure out the "how" or "when" only focuses you on the fact that what you want still hasn't arrived and only delays it from showing up. So what do you do until your desire shows up? Follow your bliss!

Years ago, when I was pursuing acting in Los Angeles, I made an attempt to help my career by contacting some former acting associates of my father's. The only semi-famous person of note was character actor Harry Dean Stanton, who had been in over 100 films, and graduated from the Pasadena Playhouse with my Dad. I had no clue as to how I'd ever meet him, but wrote his name down on my manifestation list anyway. A few months later, I stopped at a branch of my bank I normally didn't use. I was the only customer in the bank until the door opened, and in walked Harry Dean Stanton! I couldn't believe my eyes, but all I could really do was laugh. When he finished banking, I met him outside and told him who I was. He had no memory of my father whatsoever and looked at me like I was completely nuts. So much for the acting connections! Anyway, my point is that I actually crossed Harry Dean Stanton off my manifestation list.

To understand how these manifestation principles worked for me in recent times, let me take you back to the final days of living with my Mom in Temecula, and explain how everything ended up.

First of all, the relationship between my Mother and I evolved to a new level. She is an amazing woman and I clearly would have been lost without her help, as my father would have before me. I feel very fortunate to have her in my life and learned a lot from her generous, caring, loving nature. She, for the record, has adopted a much healthier lifestyle now too, and going through the changes together only strengthened our relationship all the more. She represents unconditional love better than anyone I've ever met, and has taught me many lessons my father was not capable of. Lessons like serving others, giving, helping, caring, sharing, and the overall importance of staying positive.

In April of 2013, my Mom put her house on the market, as she was downsizing to a 2-bedroom apartment. I still didn't know where I was going to end up or what I was going to do for work. This time, though, I looked forward to it because I felt much better, was no longer depressed, and finally had the ability to think and focus clearly again. Of course, being on my own and having my solitude back was something I missed a great deal and couldn't wait to retain. *I put out to the Universe a very strong desire to manifest the perfect job as well as the perfect place to live and had dogmatic faith they would both effortlessly come into fruition.*

I ended up selling a lot of things including my childhood baseball card collection, my Dad's vintage Playboy collection, and helped my Mother sell a bunch of her furniture. This would be the only money I had to get started on my own, and it would be just enough for a deposit and first month's rent in San Diego.

My Mother's house sold within 2 weeks of being on the market, so I had to find a place to live right away, and move out by May 1st.

San Diego had plenty of opportunity and the best climate anyone could ask for. I had no idea where to look for places, so turned to Craigslist and found a detached guesthouse in Mission Beach. On the way to find it, I got lost and somehow ended up in Ocean Beach.

I parked on a coastal street, got out and asked a beachgoer for directions. On my walk back, I noticed a "Now Renting" sign on a nice looking apartment building right on the beach. I called the number and the manager said a studio was available. It was kind of small, but it had a great ocean breeze and a huge back private patio. I was sold instantaneously!

The rent was $1200 a month, and again, with no job prospects on the horizon, I'd have to figure things out fast, but come hell or high water, that's what I was going to do. I took the studio and moved in on April 20, 2013, one day before my 40th birthday.

Work wise, my instinct told me I had to go back to what I had with success with in the past; sales. I looked at the classifieds, but the only thing that looked appealing to me was selling solar. After all I've said about the sun in this book, now I'd finally get to represent it for a living! Most of these jobs were straight commission, but one was offering 12 weeks of paid training, which meant a guarantee of paid rent for me. I interviewed with them and totally hit it off with the sales manager. He was a British guy with a great sense of humor and his own YouTube channel to boot. I was offered the job on the spot and accepted without hesitation. I didn't need to look elsewhere because it felt right, just like every other job I've had in my life.

I started on May 1st, 2013 and never looked back. By August, I became number one in sales and was on my way to a six-figure income! The job has given me all the freedom in the world and a first hand guided tour of San Diego and all its surrounding cities and suburbs.

I meet with residential homeowners and get 2 or 3 leads a day. Usually though, there's one in the morning and then nothing until 6 or 7pm, so there's a lot of potential downtime. That worked out perfect for me, as everyday I'd get out to the beach and bike trail and get plenty of exercise between appointments. One of my stops along my daily bike route was a jetty that was home to dozens of feral cats. I would stop there and do my Tai Chi and noticed they had a community of people that would come along and take turn feeding these cats regularly. I decided to get in on the action and bought a bag of treats with me whenever I'd visit.

95 percent of the cats wouldn't let you near them, but the other 5 percent would occasionally let you pet them. The women who fed them had names for them. There was "Junior," who was 11 years old and the oldest cat on the pier, and then there was "Pete," who would actually let me hand feed him treats right into his mouth!

It had been almost 2 years since I lost Erica, so it was nice to be in close company of felines again. I thought about adapting Pete, but he was friendly one minute, and scared to death the next. Not exactly the ideal candidate for an indoor house cat.

On July 23rd 2013, I was hand feeding Pete treats when from out of nowhere; I heard an extremely loud HISS and another cat leaped on the scene, chasing him away. It was then eyeing me up, walking in circles close to my immediate area. It almost looked like a Bengal Tiger, and for a minute I thought I was being hunted. But it was just hungry. I fed it some treats and it seemed very appreciative. It was moving too fast for me to tell if it was male or female, but when I looked at its eyes something seemed off. It almost looked cross-eyed for a second, but upon further investigation, I could see that the right eye was dead, and it could only see out of its left.

The next time I returned to the jetty, so did the one eyed cat. This time it followed me on my bike halfway up the pier, which I thought was extremely cool. I rewarded it with treats, at which point it did the figure eight around my legs and let me pet it quite a bit.

Things were a little slow initially at my sales job, but by coincidentally, the same day I met the one eyed cat, I started a major hot streak that continued all summer and into the fall. I continued my bonding with this one eyed cat and learned it was a female from one of the women I befriended who fed the cats. I would now sit on the pier and meditate next to my new good luck charm for a good 20 or 30 minutes a day, and she even trusted me enough to let me pick her up and hold her! She would scatter when people walked by; only to resurface the second they were far enough out of range. Feral or not, it became blatantly obvious what I needed to do.

On October 4th, 2013, I officially adopted "Francesca" from the jetty. All of the jetty cats have been trapped, fixed, and returned, to control population concerns and have all had their first round of shots as well. Aside from the initial shock of being taken out of her environment, there was little to no problems when I got her home. I think it had a lot to do with our relationship having already grown so strong. Without taking anything away from my beloved Erica, my bond with Francesca was even stronger, and it seemed like an instantaneous match made in heaven.

Meanwhile at work, I was kicking ass and taking names, becoming the # 1 closer in the San Diego office. I won the monthly sales contest 5 times in a row, and by the end of it, had a new flat screen TV, a juicer, a blender, an air purifier, and a food dehydrator!

All of a sudden, I found myself in a higher tax bracket and was able to build a nice chunk of change in my bank account. Prior to this point in my life, I was able to master the art of getting by with next to no money at all, so as far as I was concerned, $100,000 may have well been $100, 000, 000.

The truth is, it's not healthy to be overly attached to anything. Everything in life is a loan at best. When we die, everything we own becomes someone else's temporary possession, or is thrown away. Material possessions are a trick of the ego. As long as our essential needs are covered, a happy and healthy life can be achieved very easily without being financially "wealthy." In my opinion, wealth is not about money, but about an abundance of love and happiness.

Nevertheless, I knew having money would be the last test to find out if I truly licked the alcohol habit or not. Meaning, if you have no money to buy it with, you pretty much can't consume it anyway. This proved to me that I could think about it, be around it, afford it, and still not want it any longer. In my drinking days, I'd fantasize about having enough money to buy the best quality liquor to obtain the best quality buzz. Who ever thought I'd abandon the idea altogether in exchange for clarity of consciousness?

After a year on the job, I realized I had way more than enough saved to take some time off and work on my creative dreams. It was time for me to revisit the concept of public speaking and putting out a second book. I look forward to the challenges that public speaking will bring to the table, but more importantly, I look forward to inspiring others by spreading the message of what I've learned.

One last note about Francesca; about four

months in, I found out *she* was actually a *HE*! Once a cat is fixed, it's hard to tell the difference between male and female, and the cat feeder lady, a woman with *eight* cats of her own, told me it was female. If I can't trust her word on cat gender with confidence, who's can I? Anyway, I changed his name to Francesco and had a laugh about it with my friends and family. Male or female, I ended up with the best cat on the planet. He is the best positive addiction I could ever ask for!

As for my lifestyle change, all I can say is so far, so good. No more allergies. No more headaches. I wake up totally rested and fully alive. Ready to start my day in a positive way. I bounce out of bed now, feeling lighter than I ever have before. No more animal blood running through my veins. No more heavy metals, pesticides, herbicides, fungicides, growth hormones or antibiotics. No more sugar, preservatives, additives, caffeine, and 97 percent of the time, no booze.

I'm not a saint, but I look forward to helping others help themselves now. If there was help for me there's help for anyone. I feel lucky and blessed to be alive, and am thankful for each and every day I am given. I've learned that love is the antidote to fear, and the more you focus on becoming love, the better life gets. I have now come to know life as my best friend, and am eternally grateful that I've made it through to the other side.

It doesn't mean I spend every moment smiling and walking around in a non-stop bubble of happiness. For without dark times in our lives, we would never know would the good times felt like in the first place. Darkness is just an absence of light. The better you get at remaining positive and being in a constant state of appreciation, the more positive things you will attract in your life to appreciate.

And remember, it's not about dark times or negative experiences; it's about how you react to them. There are peaks and valleys in everyone's life. If you learn to enjoy the valleys as much as the peaks, you will be home free to a large degree. *All problems are based on perception.* ALL of them!!

Lastly, I recommend giving up any or all expectations of any kind. This way nothing or no one can ever let you down again. In a sense, you are turning over your life to God, faith, Mother Nature, or a higher power of some kind that all is perfect and is meant to be *exactly* the way it is. To be happy with any result may sound crazy at first, but the more you live this way, the more confirmation you will get from the Universe that you are on the right track, and you'll realize that we all are God essentially, and that we do *indeed* create our own realities.

I feel better now than I ever have before, and am very fortunate and blessed to have come out of my own personal hell with such an optimistic, positive outlook. It renewed my faith in the Universe, and that in the grand scheme of things, everything has always been, and always will be, ok.

Thank you for reading this book and sharing some time with me. I sincerely hope you join me in the quest for clarity of your own consciousness, overcome your own vices, and achieve joy, happiness, peace, prosperity, and love in every aspect of your life!!

ABOUT THE AUTHOR

Tyler Feneck is an author, public speaker, and all around nice guy. His background as a stand up comedian brings humor and originality to his delivery style. He lives at the beach in San Diego and enjoys spending time with his one-eyed rescue cat, Francesco. Tyler's first book, *The Cat and The Comedian* is available through his website, http://sexycomedian.com

www.ingramcontent.com/pod-product-compliance
Lightning Source LLC
LaVergne TN
LVHW021525080426
835509LV00018B/2659